DC SUPER HERO SCIENCE

BY JENNIFER HACKETT

downtown bookworks
LONDON PUBLIC LIBRARY

downtown bookworks

Downtown Bookworks Inc.
265 Canal Street
New York, NY 10013
www.downtownbookworks.com

Designed by Georgia Rucker
Printed in Canada, May 2019
ISBN 978-1-941367-53-7

10 9 8 7 6 5 4 3 2

PHOTO CREDITS 10: RS89/Shutterstock.com. 16: Baranov E/Shutterstock.com. 31: Independent birds/
Shutterstock.com. 33: Zeralein99/Shutterstock.com. 36: ©Danté Fenolio/Science Source (lanternfish, hatchetfish),
wildestanimal/Shutterstock.com (shark), boban_nz/Shutterstock.com (elephantfish). 37: Susy Baels/Shutterstock.com.
39: Photo by Heather Gerquest. 45: Joseph Sohm/Shutterstock.com. 48: Billion Photos/Shutterstock.com.
49: ©iStock.com/jamesbenet. 58–59: ONYXprj/Shutterstock.com (all). 60–61: photolinc/Shutterstock.com.
61: Triff/Shutterstock.com. 65: ©Bence Mate/NaturePL/Science Source. 67: Tono Balaguer/Shutterstock.com
(girl on left), Ievgen Repiashenko/Shutterstock.com (girl on right). 71: solar22/Shutterstock.com. 73: MarcelClemens/
Shutterstock.com. 75: Photo by U.S. Army Staff Sgt. Mark Burrell, 210th Mobile Public Affairs Detachment
(soldier's helmet); U.S. Army photo by Staff Sgt. Jerry Saslav (night vision). 77: Tiina Tuomaala/Shutterstock.com
(daylight marigold), ©Bjorn Rorslett/Science Source (UV marigold), Arnoud Quanjer/Shutterstock.com (scorpion).
81: New Africa/Shutterstock.com. 87: Mateusz Atroszko/Shutterstock.com. 89: ©Claus Lunau/Science Source
(all). 91: ©2019 BAE Systems. 95: Rost9/Shutterstock.com. 97: ©Ottobock (prosthetic hand), SeventyFour/
Shutterstock.com (prosthetic leg). 105: Steven R Smith/Shutterstock.com (poison ivy), illustrissima/Shutterstock.com
(lily of the valley), Debu55y/Shutterstock.com (hydrangea), Martin Fowler/Shutterstock.com (mistletoe). 107: Photo
by NASA. 109: ©Biosphoto/SuperStock (torbernite), ©DeAgostini/SuperStock
(cinnabar, stibnite).

ILLUSTRATION CREDITS Select illustrations by Scott Kolins: Bumblebee (pages 6–9, 86–87), Black Canary (page 44).
All activity illustrations by Georgia Rucker.

CONTENTS

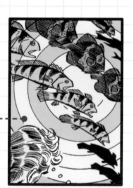

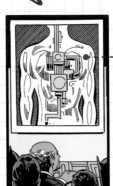

What Is SCIENCE?

Science is a way of studying the world around us using experiments and observation. There are many types of science—and many different super heroes!

Super heroes have exciting powers. Some fly through the air while others swim through the sea. Some can see through walls, and some can create weapons out of light. There are many ways that super heroes get their powers. And science can be used to understand these powers!

The SCIENTIFIC Method

Some super heroes, like Bumblebee, are also scientists. Bumblebee might use **THE SCIENTIFIC METHOD** to tackle a tricky question. The scientific method is an approach to asking questions and finding answers.

STEP 1:
MAKE AN OBSERVATION

STEP 2:
ASK A QUESTION

STEP 3:
FORM A HYPOTHESIS

STEP 4:
CONDUCT AN EXPERIMENT

STEP 5:
ANALYZE THE RESULTS

STEP 1: *MAKE AN OBSERVATION*

Bumblebee **OBSERVES** her surroundings. She uses her senses to carefully watch and listen to what happens. She notices something interesting about how a plant in sunlight grows versus how the same plant in shade grows.

STEP 2: *ASK A QUESTION*

Based on her observations, Bumblebee asks a **QUESTION** she would like an answer to. Bumblebee asks, "I wonder if sunlight makes plants grow better or worse?"

STEP 3: *FORM A HYPOTHESIS*

Bumblebee forms a **HYPOTHESIS**, an informed guess at the answer to her question. "If a plant gets sunlight," she hypothesizes, "then it will grow better than it would in the shade." A good hypothesis can be tested by an experiment. Sometimes before a hypothesis is formed, a scientist will do extra research to figure out what the best hypothesis might be.

GROWN IN SUNLIGHT

GROWN IN SHADE

STEP 4: *CONDUCT AN EXPERIMENT*

To test her hypothesis, Bumblebee carefully plans an **EXPERIMENT**. An experiment is a controlled investigation into a topic. Bumblebee decides to grow three identical plants. She puts one in sunlight, one in shade, and one in total darkness. Each plant is growing in the same soil and gets the same amount of water each day. It is important that the only difference between the plants is the amount of sunlight they get, which is what Bumblebee wants to test. Each day, she measures how tall the plants are and takes a photo to track the plants' growth.

GROWN IN SUNLIGHT

GROWN IN SHADE

GROWN IN DARKNESS

STEP 5: *ANALYZE THE RESULTS*

Bumblebee organizes the data, or information she collected during her experiment, into tables. She might turn her data into a graph to easily display and compare it. Bumblebee sees that the plant in sunlight grew the most, while the plant in darkness barely grew at all. Based on her experiment, she concludes that sunlight is important for plant growth. This **CONCLUSION** answers her hypothesis!

Sometimes an experiment shows something different than what a researcher hypothesizes. This is OK! Your conclusion doesn't need to prove your hypothesis. It just needs to be supported by research.

PHYSICS
The Building Blocks of Everything

PHYSICS is the study of matter and energy and how they interact. Physicists study things like motion, electricity, sound, and light. They also study **ATOMS**.

ATOMS are so small you can't see them, but they're everywhere. They're made of even smaller particles: protons, neutrons, and electrons. Many super heroes take advantage of the atom's unique properties. Black Lightning can generate electricity. His powers use electrons. Bumblebee and Starfire can fire energy blasts. These power bursts might be made by breaking atoms apart or supercharging them with energy!

The center of an atom is called a **NUCLEUS**. The nucleus is made up of protons and neutrons.

ELECTRONS orbit, or move around, an atom's nucleus. Electrons are always moving.

EVERYTHING FROM SUPERMAN'S CAPE TO CLARK KENT'S GLASSES TO THE WORDS ON THIS PAGE IS MADE UP OF ATOMS.

How Small Is an ATOM?

Look at the width of a single strand of your hair. Now imagine something a million times smaller. That's how big an atom is. There's no way to see an atom without a very special microscope.

After a lab experiment, scientist Ray Palmer gained the ability to shrink himself down to the size of, well, an atom or even one of the particles that makes up an atom! As the super hero the Atom, he can also become the size of a bottle or shrink so small that a diamond ring fits over his arm. His small size lets him sneak around undetected.

No matter what size the Atom is, he still has the same mass, or number of atoms. That means that, when he is small, there's an incredible number of atoms in an extremely tiny space. His superpower lets him jump incredibly high and punch with surprising force. All the force behind his punch is packed into a point smaller than the tip of your pencil!

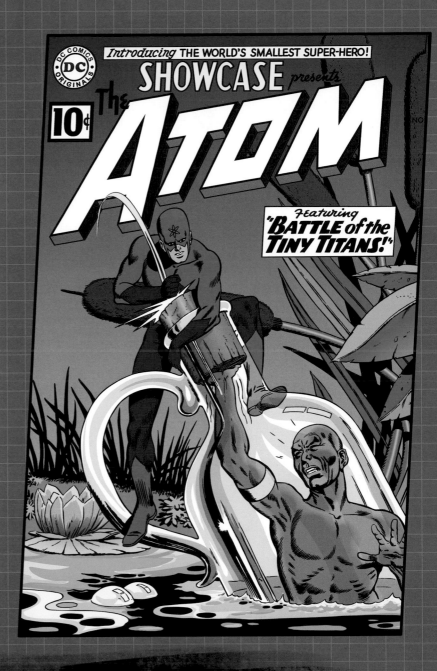

HE'S VERY POWERFUL, BUT HE CAN BE INCREDIBLY TINY. SO PLEASE, TRY NOT TO STEP ON THE ATOM!

SCIENTIST SPOTLIGHT

THE ATOM, PHYSICIST

Raymond "Ray" Palmer was a **PHYSICIST** before he became the Atom. Physicists are experts in physics, the study of matter, forces, and energy. They work to understand what makes up the universe. Some physicists study atoms. By crashing atoms together at very high speeds, physicists can learn more about what makes up our world.

Other physicists want to understand how things interact, from cars to planets. They look at how the forces between objects can push, pull, and move things. This lets them predict how planets millions of miles away from us move. Or it lets them help build things like planes and roller coasters safely. There are many ways to be a physicist!

Physicists like Ray Palmer know that there is energy in all things—
even a chair sitting on the ground. There are two types of energy:
KINETIC ENERGY and **POTENTIAL ENERGY**. Kinetic energy is the energy
something has due to motion. The Flash running and an arrow soaring
through the air have kinetic energy. Potential energy is stored
energy. A ball held up in the air and a coiled
spring have potential energy.

ROLLER COASTERS start by climbing a huge hill to build up potential energy. When the roller coaster zooms down the hill, the potential energy becomes kinetic energy. And this energy carries the coaster through the entire track—no engine needed! A physicist helps design a roller coaster by finding out how much potential energy the coaster needs to finish the track safely.

What Is GRAVITY?

There are forces working all the time. One of those forces is **GRAVITY**. Just like a force field, gravity is invisible, but it is very important. It is a force that pulls objects together.

Every object has gravity. But the biggest, heaviest objects have the most gravity. The biggest object on Earth is...well, Earth. It is Earth's strong gravitational pull that keeps the moon orbiting around Earth. The sun's gravitational pull is much stronger than Earth's. It keeps Earth and the other planets orbiting around the sun.

EARTH'S GRAVITY KEEPS THE MOON IN ORBIT.

Belts made of Nth Metal

GRAVITY-DEFYING MATERIALS DON'T EXIST ON EARTH, BUT THEY DO IN COMICS. NTH METAL, FOUND ON THE PLANET THANAGAR, HAS THE POWER TO CANCEL OUT GRAVITY. HAWKMAN AND HAWKGIRL WEAR BELTS MADE OF NTH METAL. THAT'S WHY THEY CAN FLY.

When you jump up, you always land back on the ground. Why? Because Earth's gravity is pulling you to it. **Go ahead. Try it. Jump up, up, up as high as you can.** You land back on the ground, right?

UP, UP, AND AWAY!

Super heroes are pulled by gravity too. When Superman leaps over a huge building, he is eventually pulled back to Earth. But he is so much stronger than the average person—and he can fly—so Superman can jump up higher and stay in the air longer than other people or flying animals.

AND . . . EVEN SUPERMAN COMES BACK TO EARTH THANKS TO GRAVITY.

How Do Arrows FLY?

Green Arrow never misses a shot. That's because he's an expert at **PROJECTILE MOTION!** Projectile motion is how objects move after being launched into an arc. Green Arrow has to understand a few key physics terms to always hit his mark: velocity, acceleration, and gravity. **VELOCITY** is how fast something is moving in a specific direction.

INITIAL VELOCITY is how fast a projectile (the arrow) is going before acceleration or other forces cause it to change speed.

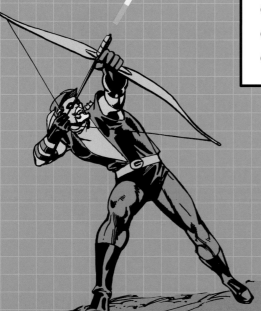

To shoot something, especially something far away, Green Arrow aims upward. By shooting upward, the arrow will travel in an arc. It can fly higher and farther before gravity pulls it back to the ground.

ACCELERATION is how much the velocity of the projectile changes over a certain amount of time.

FORCE DUE TO GRAVITY is the pull on an object toward the ground caused by gravity.

FINAL VELOCITY is how fast the projectile is going after it's been changed by acceleration or other forces.

When Green Arrow shoots an arrow, the force of gravity acts on it and pulls it toward the ground. If he shoots straight at a target that is far away, gravity will probably make him miss his mark.

Can You
PHASE THROUGH
Walls?

Martian Manhunter is from another world. He has many powers, including flying and the ability to read people's minds. He can also walk through walls. He does this by phasing through them—that means he moves his atoms in the spaces between the atoms of the wall.

Both the wall and Martian Manhunter are examples of **MATTER**. Matter is anything that is made of atoms or anything that has mass and takes up space.

There are three types of matter.

GASES spread across wide distances and have no set shape. The distance between the atoms that make up a gas can be huge! We can easily move through gases because the atoms are so spread out.

The air around us is made up of a mixture of gases. Humans can walk right through them. Batgirl has no trouble running through the air.

LIQUIDS take on the shape of their container. Think of a cup of water or bowl of soup. Their atoms are more closely connected, but they aren't stiff and rigid. It takes more effort to move through a liquid than to move through a gas.

People can swim through liquids such as water. The Flash can too!

The atoms in **SOLIDS** are closely connected in a defined shape. Unlike Martian Manhunter, humans can't move through solids—the atoms are just too close together!

People can't move through solids like they can through air or liquids. But, like Batman, they can smash through solids if they are strong enough!

How Hot Is HEAT VISION?

Superman's heat vision is really hot! He can even melt metal with an intense stare. But why do things melt in the first place?

Melting is a **PHASE CHANGE**. A phase change is when one state of matter changes into another state, such as when a liquid freezes and becomes a solid.

It's lucky for Batman and Robin that ice can undergo a phase change! When the ice melts back into a liquid, the Dynamic Duo will be free—and ready to go after the chilly villain Mr. Freeze!

Once, Superman's heat vision went haywire. He melted his own glasses!

Melting an object changes it from a solid to a liquid. When something heats up, its atoms are excited and start to move. Eventually, the distance between atoms grows, which causes a solid to lose its rigid shape and begin to shift around. That's when the object melts. The atoms start to move because **HEAT** is a type of energy. When Superman uses his heat vision on an object, he's giving it a huge blast of energy!

If Superman can melt steel with his gaze, that means his heat vision reaches at least 2,500 degrees Fahrenheit.

FAHRENHEIT is a measure of temperature. On the Fahrenheit scale, water freezes at 32 degrees and boils at 212 degrees. Another common temperature scale is Celsius. On the Celsius scale, water freezes at 0 degrees and boils at 100 degrees.

WHAT FALLS FASTEST?

The force of gravity always pulls things back to the ground. It's why when you throw a ball in the air it always comes back down! But does the weight of an object change how it falls? Let's find out.

MATERIALS:

Yardstick or other type of measuring device

Beanbag

Feather

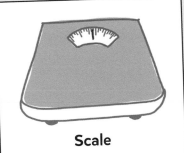

Scale

Bottle cap

1. Weigh the beanbag, the bottle cap, and the feather. Record the weight of each object. Write a hypothesis about which you think will hit the ground first when dropped.

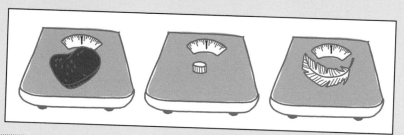

2. Hold the beanbag in one hand and the bottle cap in the other. Make sure they're at the same height! (You could also have a friend or adult do this step so you can better observe what happens.)

3. Drop the beanbag and the bottle cap at the exact same time from the same height. Watch to see which touches the ground first. Are you surprised?

4. Drop the beanbag and the feather at the exact same time from the same height. Watch to see which touches the ground first. Are you surprised?

What's Happening? Weight has no impact on the force of gravity. Gravity pulls all objects back to the ground at the exact same speed, so a heavy object falls just as fast as a lightweight one! If the feather fell slower than the beanbag or the bottle cap, it's because it is less **AERODYNAMIC**. This means that air catches on it and slows its fall. There are many factors that impact how things move!

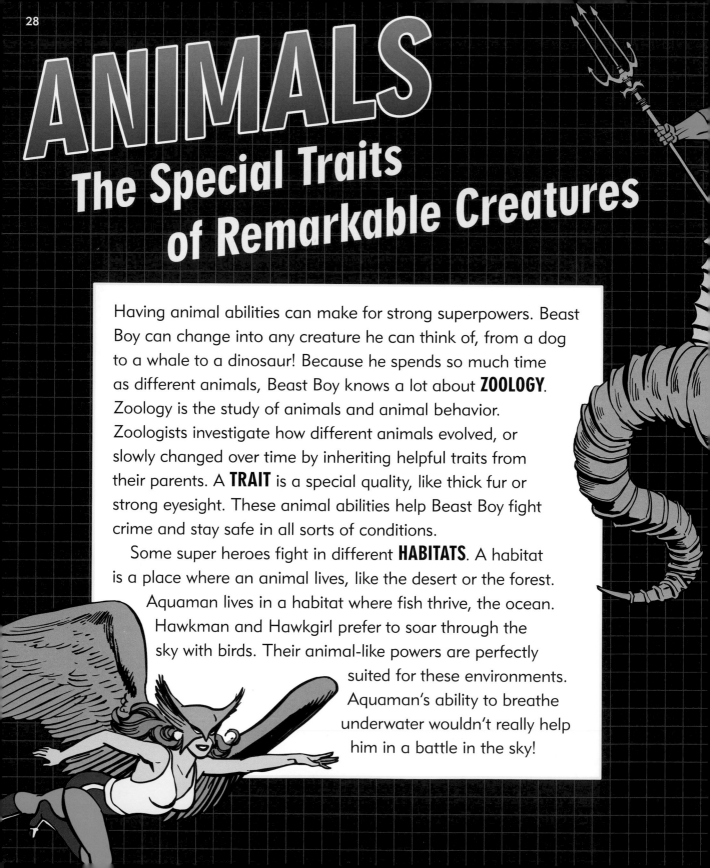

ANIMALS

The Special Traits of Remarkable Creatures

Having animal abilities can make for strong superpowers. Beast Boy can change into any creature he can think of, from a dog to a whale to a dinosaur! Because he spends so much time as different animals, Beast Boy knows a lot about **ZOOLOGY**. Zoology is the study of animals and animal behavior. Zoologists investigate how different animals evolved, or slowly changed over time by inheriting helpful traits from their parents. A **TRAIT** is a special quality, like thick fur or strong eyesight. These animal abilities help Beast Boy fight crime and stay safe in all sorts of conditions.

Some super heroes fight in different **HABITATS**. A habitat is a place where an animal lives, like the desert or the forest. Aquaman lives in a habitat where fish thrive, the ocean. Hawkman and Hawkgirl prefer to soar through the sky with birds. Their animal-like powers are perfectly suited for these environments. Aquaman's ability to breathe underwater wouldn't really help him in a battle in the sky!

How Do Birds FLY?

Hawkman and Hawkgirl soar through the air using their large wings. They can fly just like birds! But how do birds actually fly? It isn't just by flapping!

Hawkman and Hawkgirl's wing shape makes all the difference. Like regular birds, their wings have a special shape. The top of their wings is slightly sloped, so air traveling over the top of their wings has to travel farther than air passing under the bottom of their wings. When air travels over the top side of the wing, it has to rush by faster to cover the longer distance.

This creates a difference in **AIR PRESSURE** that keeps fliers in the air. Air pressure is the force exerted on objects by the air around them.

Birds flap their wings to get moving and to get air flowing over their wings! Air passing over wings travels farther and faster than air passing under wings.

AIR

AIR

As the air speeds up, it creates a pocket of **lower air pressure** on top of the wing. The **higher pressure** on the bottom of the wing pushes the bird—or the super hero—up into the air.

How Do Fish Breathe UNDERWATER?

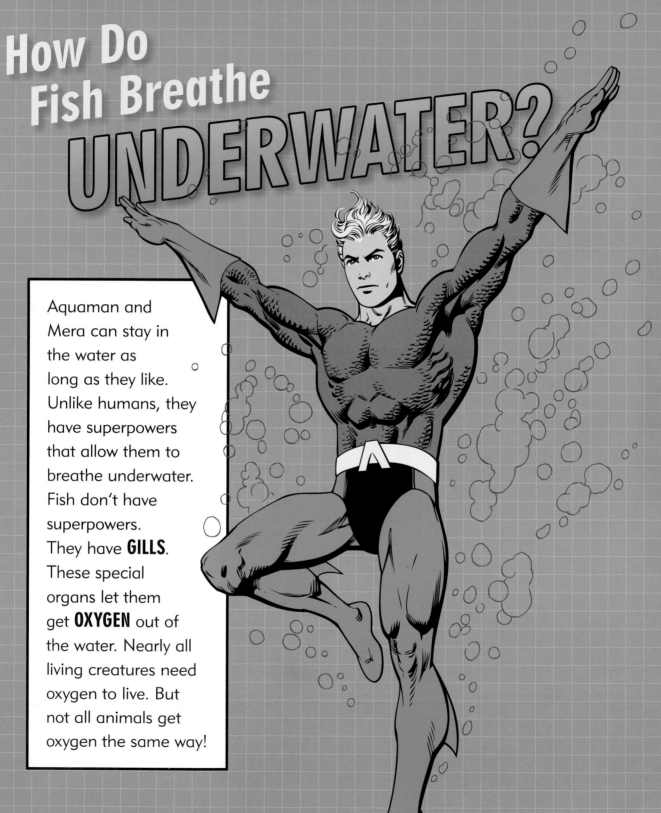

Aquaman and Mera can stay in the water as long as they like. Unlike humans, they have superpowers that allow them to breathe underwater. Fish don't have superpowers. They have **GILLS**. These special organs let them get **OXYGEN** out of the water. Nearly all living creatures need oxygen to live. But not all animals get oxygen the same way!

When humans breathe, we inhale air, and our **LUNGS** expand. This pulls air down our windpipe and into our lungs. The lungs transfer oxygen into our blood and remove harmful carbon dioxide. The oxygen-rich blood is pumped through our bodies by our heart. It keeps our organs healthy. When we exhale, carbon dioxide from the air is released.

Fish need oxygen too. But they don't have lungs! Instead, they take water into their mouths. Water is made up of hydrogen and oxygen. Fish have a special way to get the oxygen that's contained in water. When water flows over their gills, the gills let in oxygen but not water. The oxygen moves into their blood, and the water passes through.

A FISH'S GILLS

Can You COMMUNICATE with Sea Creatures?

As the rulers of the sea, Aquaman and Mera are happy underwater. They can even communicate with fish.

Aquaman uses his **TELEPATHIC** powers to send messages with his mind to the fish he wants to talk to. And a big group of fish is a mighty foe!

"I MET A *DORADO* FLEEING FROM THE ALIEN CREATURE WHICH HAD EMERGED FROM THE METEOR..."

BEWARE, *AQUAMAN!* OUR OCEAN BROTHERS HAVE BEEN TURNED TO *GLASS!* ONLY I--THE *DORADO*-- BECAUSE I CAN SWIM SO FAST, ESCAPED THAT TERRIBLE FATE!

Once, to defeat an alien that was turning all the creatures in the sea into glass, Aquaman asked his finny friends to make noise. Fish do make noises (and not just in comic books). Many types of fish, like the gurnard and the toadfish, make noises that range from clicks, pops, groans, and grunts to whistles, purrs, barks, and growls. They make sounds by vibrating their **SWIM BLADDER**, which is a gas-filled sac that helps fish float.

Humans can't send messages with our minds. But fish can and do communicate with one another without words. They swim together in large organized groups, called schools. They stay in sync by gesturing. Some special fish can even create electrical pulses or make parts of their body glow to communicate!

HMM... ALL DEEP-WATER FISH POSSESS LUMINESCENT ORGANS WHICH MAKE THEM SHINE IN THE DARK... LIKE THOSE HATCHETFISH AND LANTERNFISH!

LANTERNFISH contain luciferin, a molecule that makes light when it reacts with oxygen. Their light may help them find mates.

Like lanternfish, **HATCHETFISH** have light-producing organs called photophores along their undersides. Scientists think they try to glow like the water above them, so predators won't see them from below.

SHARKS have nasal cavities, but they're not for breathing! They sniff the water they swim through to pick up on the scent of prey or possible mates.

ELEPHANTFISH send and receive electrical pulses. They use these signals to warn their friends about predators or dangerous conditions.

Some aquatic creatures, like dolphins, are very smart. Humans can train them to perform tricks for tasty treats! We can't talk to them with our minds, but we can speak to dolphins using hand signals and whistles.

HUMANS CAN COMMUNICATE WITH DOLPHINS WITHOUT SUPERPOWERS.

Can Dogs TALK?

PULL THE CHAIN, KRYPTO!

Superman has a very special pet friend—Krypto the Super-Dog! Krypto can fly and use many of the same powers Superman has. He's also very intelligent. He thinks in sentences and understands Superman's orders perfectly even if he can't always control his super-strength!

Normal dogs aren't quite so smart. They don't think in words like humans do, and they don't understand complicated sentences. But that doesn't mean they can't learn! Many dog breeds can learn basic commands. Some breeds, like German shepherds and border collies, can learn to perform complicated tasks. These working dogs are their own kind of super hero, sniffing out bombs or helping their human owners stay safe as service dogs.

THIS CLEVER DOG MIGHT NOT BE ABLE TO SAY "YOU'RE WELCOME!" BUT SHE CAN STILL GET THE DOOR FOR YOU!

DESIGN SUPER HERO SIDEKICKS

ACTIVITY

There are many types of animals in the world. Some are aquatic, which means they live in water. Some are mammals that have hair or fur and breathe air. Most mammals live on land. Some animals are amphibians— they live both in water and on land! Different animals are best for different types of jobs. Think of all of the animals you know and what makes them special. Design an animal sidekick for each super hero. What would be the perfect pet friend to keep up with their heroics?

MATERIALS:

Construction paper

Markers or colored pencils

Optional: Additional craft supplies, such as pipe cleaners, pom-poms, string, etc.

1. What kind of powerful pet would be best for high-flying Hawkgirl?

2. What sidekick would Aquaman love? Would it live with him in the water?

3. Batman is most active at night. What kind of creature would make a good sidekick?

4. Wonder Woman is always on the go. What kind of pet should she have?

5. Draw or create an animal for Hawkgirl, Aquaman, Batman, and Wonder Woman. Explain why you chose each creature.

What Were You Thinking? Did you match each sidekick's traits to its super hero partner? Which traits did you focus on for each super hero? Maybe you gave Hawkgirl a bird that could fly alongside her, Aquaman an aquatic animal that could breathe underwater, and Batman a creature that can see in the dark. How did you decide which animal should accompany Wonder Woman on her adventures?

WAVES
The Power of Moving Energy

In science, **WAVES** are very important. But the waves scientists talk about aren't like the ones we use to say hello or the ones you see in the ocean. These waves are the transfer of energy from one place to another. Light and sound are examples of waves. You can't see these waves, but they're incredibly powerful.

Cyborg has a sonic cannon on his arm that uses sound waves as a weapon to stun his enemies. It's strong enough to shatter rock or bend metal.

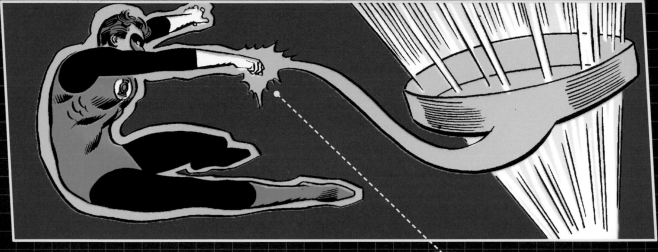

Many powers are types of waves. Super heroes like Cyborg and Black Canary use sound waves, or sonic waves, to fight their enemies. Green Lantern uses light, which is a type of wave, every time he uses his ring.

Waves can be used for more than fighting too. Every time Batman answers a call on a radio, makes a video call using a satellite, or picks up a cell phone, he's using radio waves to communicate. From combat to conversation, waves can do it all!

Green Lantern can create objects, weapons, and force fields out of green light.

What Are WAVES?

Energy is transferred from one place to another by waves. There are two main types of waves.

1. MECHANICAL WAVES need a medium, or some matter, to travel through. That medium is usually air or water. The molecules that make up the medium move and pass on energy to the molecules next to them, which lets the wave travel. Sound waves are mechanical waves. Seismic waves—the waves that cause earthquakes—are also mechanical waves.

When two or more atoms bond together, they create **MOLECULES.** Everything around you is made up of molecules. A water molecule is made up of two hydrogen atoms and one oxygen atom. That's why water is known as H_2O.

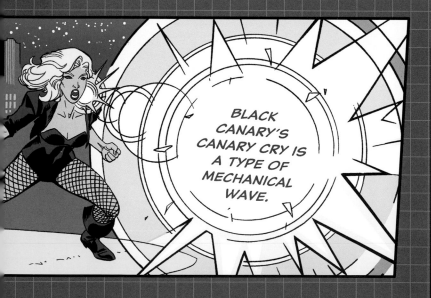

BLACK CANARY'S CANARY CRY IS A TYPE OF MECHANICAL WAVE.

2. ELECTROMAGNETIC WAVES don't need anything to travel through. They include all types of light and X-rays. They're caused by the vibration of charged particles rather than an initial movement.

Mechanical waves are started by an initial movement that sets off the wave. They can move in different ways depending on how the source of the wave moved to begin with. It all depends on whether the original motion was up and down or left and right.

LONGITUDINAL WAVES move in a straight line from left to right or right to left. They happen when the initial wave motion was from side to side.

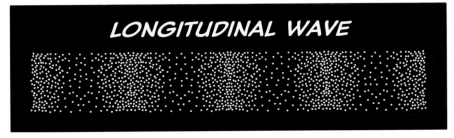

LONGITUDINAL WAVE

TRANSVERSE WAVES move up and down like a squiggly line. They happen when the initial wave motion was up and down.

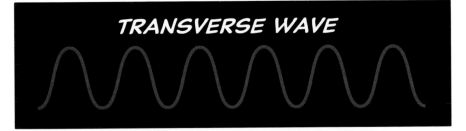

TRANSVERSE WAVE

When fans do the wave at a football or baseball game, they're making a transverse wave!

Can Your VOICE Break Things?

Whenever you talk, you produce **SOUND WAVES**. People hear when these waves reach their eardrums, which translate the sound waves into words, music, and other noises. Black Canary can talk, just like you or me. She can also produce a sonic scream, which is a high-powered wave of sound. Black Canary's Canary Cry can shatter objects and stop villains in their tracks!

A **SONIC WAVE** is an incredibly powerful kind of pressure wave. The normal human body can't produce high enough pitches to create this kind of wave. But that doesn't mean it doesn't exist! High-powered sonic devices have been used as burglar deterrents, by the military, and in the lab to incapacitate people and, yes, shatter glass.

All waves have a **FREQUENCY** and a **WAVELENGTH**. Frequency is how many times the wave repeats itself in one second. Wavelength is the distance between peaks on a wave. These two qualities can tell you a lot about a sound wave. A low-pitched sound has a longer wavelength and a lower frequency. Higher-pitched sounds have shorter wavelengths and higher frequencies. What do you think Black Canary's sonic wave looks like?

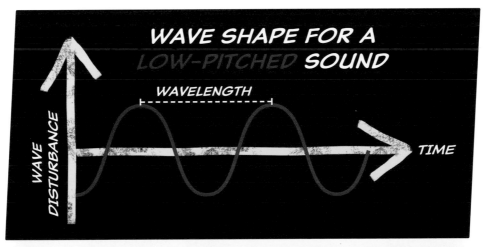

WAVE SHAPE FOR A LOW-PITCHED SOUND

WAVELENGTH

WAVE DISTURBANCE

TIME

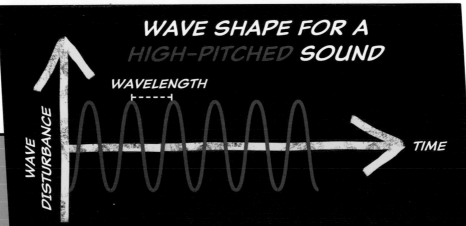

WAVE SHAPE FOR A HIGH-PITCHED SOUND

WAVELENGTH

WAVE DISTURBANCE

TIME

Can a Person Stop an EARTHQUAKE?

Earthquakes happen when rock suddenly moves or breaks within the planet. They cause **SEISMIC WAVES** that move Earth's layers, shaking the ground.

The **CRUST** is the solid outer layer of the planet. People live and build on Earth's crust.

The **MANTLE** is a rocky layer that makes up about 85% of the weight of Earth.

The **OUTER CORE** is a liquid layer made of molten rock and metals.

The **INNER CORE** is the center of the planet. It is a solid ball of metal (mostly iron and nickel).

Small seismic waves are always traveling through Earth. But when there's a sudden break or movement, a large amount of energy is released. The **MAGNITUDE** of an earthquake determines how strong it is. It's a measure of the seismic energy released.

To stop an earthquake, you would need to take all the energy out of the ground to stop the wave from traveling. That isn't a problem for Superman, but scientists haven't figured out how to do that yet—that's a LOT of energy to absorb!

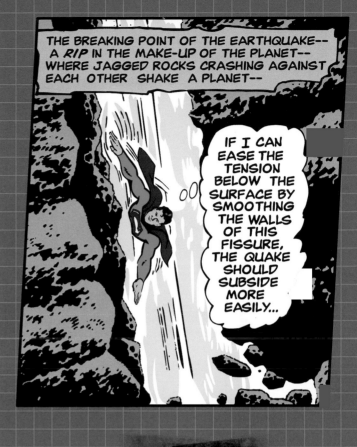

THE BREAKING POINT OF THE EARTHQUAKE-- A *RIP* IN THE MAKE-UP OF THE PLANET-- WHERE JAGGED ROCKS CRASHING AGAINST EACH OTHER SHAKE A PLANET--

IF I CAN EASE THE TENSION BELOW THE SURFACE BY SMOOTHING THE WALLS OF THIS FISSURE, THE QUAKE SHOULD SUBSIDE MORE EASILY...

Seismic waves are recorded by a **SEISMOGRAPH.** Super heroes and intergalactic troublemakers can set off earthquakes during their battles. And humans can cause seismic waves when mining, building dams, or setting off large explosions that send energy through Earth. Big groups of people jumping up and down have caused a seismograph to record a wave—but they haven't caused any earthquakes!

Can You Make Things Out of LIGHT?

Green Lantern's powerful ring lets him make weapons out of light. Anything he can think of, he can create! And his amazing light constructs pack a punch (he can even make an enormous green fist out of light!). People without superpowers can't do what Green Lantern can do. But what can we do with light?

ZAP! In comics, **LASERS** are often used as powerful superweapons, but in real life they're much more practical. A laser is a concentrated beam of light. Light is made up of particles called **PHOTONS**. Lasers are stronger and brighter than regular light because they're made of very organized lines of photons. They travel farther than regular light because the energy from the laser constantly generates new photons.

If you've ever used a laser pointer or a DVD player, then you've seen a low-energy laser in action. Other types of lasers have a lot of energy! These lasers can be used for surgery or to cut very small patterns into metal.

Lasers and visible light all fall under the study of **OPTICS**. Scientists who study optics learn all about the behavior of light. Green Lantern probably knows a lot about optics to make the most of his powers!

A flashlight shines visible light. It isn't very focused, so the light spreads out and doesn't travel that far. But a laser is very focused and orderly. It's also made up of only one color of light. That means a laser can travel in a tight line for a long distance!

 **ACTIVITY**

SEEING WAVES

Want to make some waves like Black Canary? All you need is a friend and a Slinky, and you'll be seeing waves in no time!

MATERIALS:

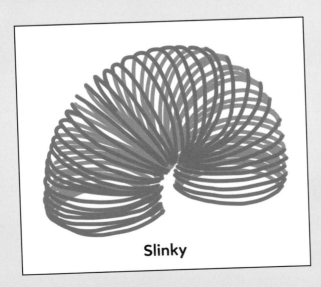

Slinky

Friend or parent

1. Hold one end of the Slinky. Have your friend or parent hold the other. Stretch the Slinky until it's mostly straight. (But make

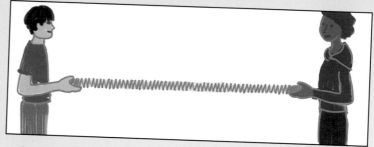

sure you don't stretch it so far that the Slinky coils get bent out of shape.) Ask your friend or parent to hold the other end of the Slinky still. What will happen if you move your end?

2. Move your end of the Slinky up and down. You've created a wave! What happens when the wave reaches the other side?

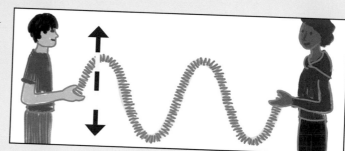

3. Push and pull the Slinky continuously back and forth while holding it level. Make sure your friend holds the other end still. What happens when the wave reaches the other side?

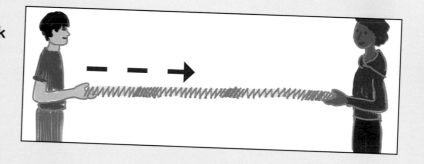

What's Happening? Using your Slinky, you've created a wave! When you move your end of the Slinky up and down, you are making a transverse wave like a light wave traveling through the air. When you push and pull the Slinky back and forth (while mostly holding it still), you are creating a longitudinal wave, like a sound wave.

Because waves are moving energy, they don't just stop but instead fade over time as the molecules return to a calmer state. When the wave reaches your friend or parent, it should reflect, or bounce back, toward you. See how long you can make your wave last!

WAVE WATCH

Seismographs detect seismic waves rippling through the earth. You can make a simple one to keep an eye out for earthquakes!

EARTHQUAKE-- IN SAN FRANCISCO...

...AND IT'S A BIGGIE!

MATERIALS:

A cereal box

Piece of paper

Yarn or string

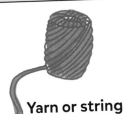

Rice

Disposable cup

Tape

Ruler

Pencil

Scissors

Make sure there is an ADULT nearby to help with some of the cuts.

Optional: Popsicle stick, hole punch

1. Tape the top of a cereal box closed. Use a ruler to measure and draw a rectangle 1 inch from the top and side edges and 2 inches from the bottom edge of the front of the cereal box. Repeat on the back of the cereal box.

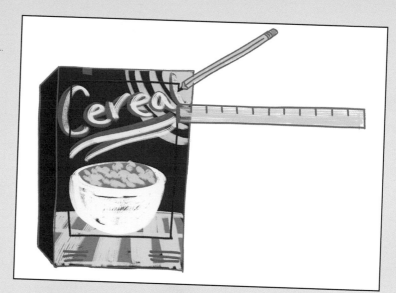

2. Cut out the rectangles you drew.

3. On the bottom border of the front of your cereal box, cut a 2-inch-long slit. Cut another 2-inch slit on the bottom of the back of the cereal box.

continued on next page

continued from previous page

4. Cut the sheet of paper into strips a little less than 2 inches wide. Feed one strip of paper through the slits in the cereal box. Set aside the other strips.

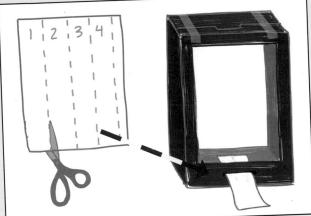

5. Have an adult punch two holes on opposite sides of the top of the cup.

6. Have an adult punch a hole through the center of the bottom of your disposable cup. Push the pencil through this hole. Tape the pencil in place, and tape the hole closed.

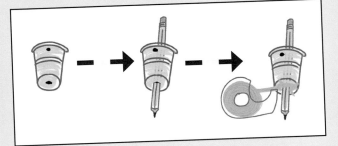

7. Fill the cup with an inch or two of rice. This will help hold the pencil in place.

8. Have an adult punch a hole in the center of the top of the cereal box.

9. Cut two pieces of yarn, about 14 inches long. Make a knot in the end of each piece of yarn. Push a piece of yarn through each hole in the cup. Pull the yarn through the hole in the top of the cereal box.

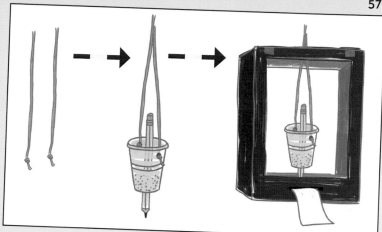

10. Adjust the yarn so the tip of the pencil just touches the strip of paper. Once you have your yarn at the right length, tie the pieces together and tape them to the top of the cereal box. (If the knotted yarn slips through the hole, place a popsicle stick or other object between the hole and the knot.)

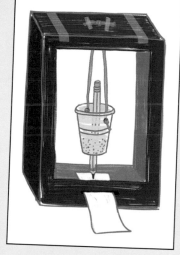

11. Place your seismograph on a table or a large piece of cardboard. Have a friend or adult slowly pull the strip of paper through while you wiggle the table or cardboard and see what happens!

What's Happening? The motion of the table moves the paper back and forth under the suspended pencil. The result is a wavy, jagged line that shows how the table moved! Real seismographs use a heavy weight suspended in the air, so Earth's seismic waves only move the base of the seismograph (and not the hanging weight or pencil). That way they can measure earthquakes more accurately.

Try your seismograph on other surfaces. Put it on a sofa cushion. Have a friend or adult pull the paper while you gently tap on the sofa cushion. Tap a little harder. Do you see a difference in the pencil markings?

POWERFUL BODIES

Anatomy of a Hero—and You!

BRAIN

Whenever you run, jump, or read, you're using your body. Our bodies are made up of muscles, bones, and organs. Super heroes have enhanced bodies, but many of them have the same basic **ANATOMY**, or body parts and structure, as we do. Their bodies are just more powerful than ours!

Our bodies need certain things to survive. We need oxygen, which we get through our lungs. We need nutrients from food that are absorbed by our intestines. And we need to be active to keep our muscles strong. Even if you aren't a super hero, it's important to keep your body in good shape!

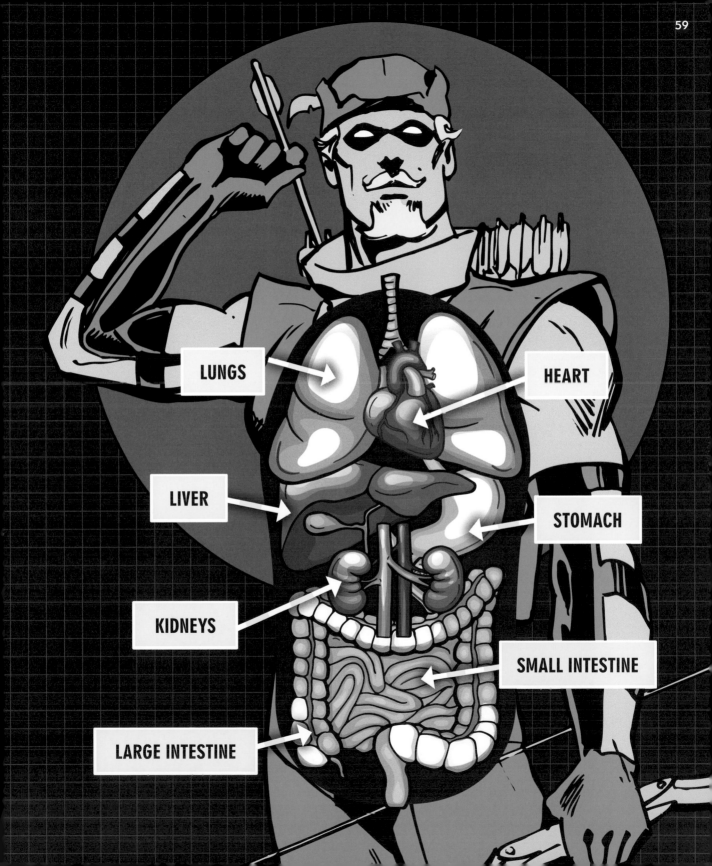

Do We Need SUNLIGHT?

Starfire loves the sun. She absorbs energy from the sun, which allows her to fly at supersonic speeds. The sun's energy also gives her strength and charges up her star bolts. Without it, she wouldn't be able to fly or fight.

Starfire is an alien, but humans need the sun too. Sunlight is a great source of vitamin D, which is important for our health. It provides energy to our ecosystem. Without the sun, we wouldn't be able to grow food! The sun also helps keep temperatures livable for humans. If the sun were farther away, Earth would be too cold. The sun's heat keeps us from freezing and keeps plants growing. Time to catch some rays (but don't forget the sunscreen!).

Earth is in a "Goldilocks Zone." It's not too hot and not too cold—it's just right!

How STRONG Is Superman?

With his strong **MUSCLES**, Superman can lift buildings, stop trains, snap iron chains, and leap for miles. Muscles are bands of tissue within the body that can expand and contract. They're like rubber bands in your body. You move your arms and legs by contracting and relaxing your muscles. They pull on your bones and make you move!

Muscles also help you lift things. When you use a muscle over and over, it gets stronger. Stronger muscles are sturdier. They can lift heavier objects or support running for longer periods of time. The average human can lift about half their body weight. Some athletes can lift several times their body weight after lots of training. But Superman can lift hundreds of times his weight—he has incredible muscles!

The heaviest weight ever lifted by a human was 6,270 pounds—an incredible feat—but still nothing compared to a 400,000-pound train!

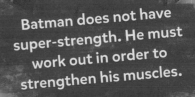

Like Superman, Wonder Woman has super-strength. A speeding train is no match for her either!

Batman does not have super-strength. He must work out in order to strengthen his muscles.

Can People Really Run ON WATER?

How fast can you run? Maybe you can run a mile in 8 minutes. That's pretty speedy, but The Flash is faster! The Flash can run about 700 miles per hour—that's almost 12 miles a minute. If you ran a mile in 8 minutes, The Flash would have finished 96 miles in the same amount of time! And that isn't even The Flash's top speed. When he really puts his mind to it, The Flash can run faster than **THE SPEED OF LIGHT**. That means he can run faster than you can see—at hundreds of millions of miles per hour!

Outside of comics, light moves faster than anything in the universe! When there are no other forces to slow it down, light travels at 186,282 miles per second! It travels a little more slowly through air or water.

The Flash can run so fast he can actually run across water. Water is a liquid. It is not firm like a solid. If you tried to step on the surface of water, you'd fall right in! But, when he runs, The Flash moves faster than water atoms can move. He's already a few steps away by the time the force of his steps causes the water to shift! The Flash needs to run at least 67 miles per hour to bounce across the water like he does. The theoretical fastest speed for a human? Forty miles per hour. Guess we'll leave walking on water to The Flash—and to the lizards!

Like The Flash, the basilisk lizard is known for running across the surface of water.

Can a Human Be as STRETCHY as Plastic Man?

Some people are very flexible. They can put their feet behind their head or do the splits. But Plastic Man takes flexibility to a whole new level. He can stretch his body to extreme lengths. He can squeeze into small spaces or wrap himself around things like a blanket. He can even use himself as a slingshot to launch things into the air!

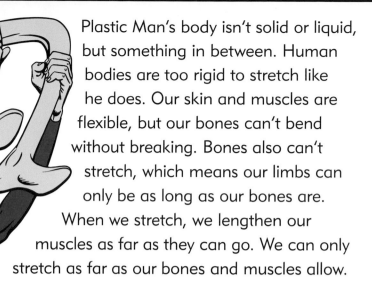

Plastic Man's body isn't solid or liquid, but something in between. Human bodies are too rigid to stretch like he does. Our skin and muscles are flexible, but our bones can't bend without breaking. Bones also can't stretch, which means our limbs can only be as long as our bones are. When we stretch, we lengthen our muscles as far as they can go. We can only stretch as far as our bones and muscles allow.

The amount that one joint or body part moves is known as its **range of motion**.

People who can bend their joints or body parts beyond the normal range of motion have **hypermobility** (but they still aren't as flexible as Plastic Man!).

MODEL MUSCLES

Flex your arm. What do you think is happening under your skin? Your arm is a series of muscles and bones working together to move. To see it in action, why not build your own arm model?

MATERIALS:

3 cardboard tubes (paper towel tubes)

Scissors

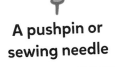

Marker

A pushpin or sewing needle

5 rubber bands

1 long paper clip, unfolded

1. Cut about 1 inch off the end of two of the cardboard tubes. Label one "radius." Label the other "ulna." Label the longest cardboard tube "humerus." Those are the names of the three large arm bones.

2. Line up the cardboard tubes. Make a dot on both sides of one end of each tube. Using the pushpin or sewing needle, poke holes through each of the dots. (Ask an adult for help if you need it.)

3. Insert the straightened-out paper clip through all six holes. Bend the edges of the paper clip on each side of the tubes.

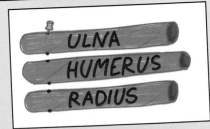

4. Wrap a rubber band around the end of the radius and ulna to keep them together.

5. Make a cut in each of the four remaining rubber bands, so they are long pieces of elastic.

6. Tie rubber band **A** tightly around the humerus, about 1 inch from the end. Tie rubber band **B** around both the radius and ulna, about 1 inch from the humerus.

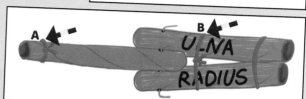

7. Set the carboard tubes up at a right angle. Tie one end of rubber band **C** to rubber band **A**. Then tie the other end to rubber band **B**.

8. Tie one end of rubber band **D** to rubber band **A** (on the opposite side from rubber band **C**). Pull it around the back of the humerus and tie the other end to rubber band **B** (on the opposite side from rubber band **C**).

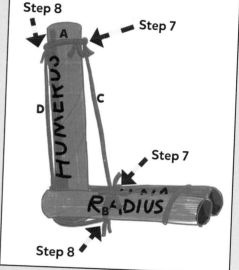

9. Move the carboard arm around and see what happens to the long rubber bands! Bend and straighten the arm to see how muscles move.

What's Happening? The cardboard tubes provide structure to your arm model (like bones). The long rubber bands stretch and relax as the bones move (like muscles). Many muscles work in pairs to push and pull bones. When one muscle stretches, its counterpart will contract, and vice versa.

If you want to see how the arm works to pick something up, attach a hooked paper clip to the end of the radius or ulna. Attach hooked paper clips to objects with different weights. Use the arm to fish up the objects and see how the rubber bands move.

INCREDIBLE EYES
How Humans and Super Heroes See

Many super heroes have special types of vision. Others use tools that help them see in special ways. Using X-ray vision, Superman and Supergirl can see through walls. Some heroes, like Martian Manhunter, can even see ultraviolet light, which lets them see colors human eyes can't! Batman uses goggles that allow him to see in the dark. But how do humans see in the first place?

Human eyes turn light into images. Light bounces off an object—a flower, a friend's face, or even this book—and into your eyes.

The light passes through the **CORNEA**, the transparent covering of your eye. As light passes through the cornea, it bends slightly.

The light bends again as it passes through your eye's **LENS**.

The lens focuses the light onto the **RETINA**, a thin layer that contains millions of light-sensing nerve cells called rods and cones. These rods and cones translate the light into colors, shapes, and other details.

The thickness of your cornea and lens determine what kind of light you can see. Some types of light have waves that are too short. They can't get through. Your rods and cones determine what colors you can see.

Can You SEE THROUGH Walls?

Sometimes heroes need to know what lies behind a wall or other type of barrier. That's no problem for Superman! He can use his X-ray vision to see through anything. With this superpower, he can quickly know how many people are in a room or if a powerful weapon is hidden in a bag.

Superman can see through walls by using **X-RAYS**. X-rays are a type of radiation with a very short wavelength. This type of radiation can pass through things like skin or cloth. It has a harder time passing through bone or solid objects though. If an X-ray detector is placed behind something—or someone—being exposed to X-rays, a picture of what's inside is formed. You might even have seen an X-ray of yourself if you've ever broken a bone!

MY *X-RAY VISION* REVEALS NOTHING AGAIN....!

HOLD IT! I JUST REALIZED-- I'M NOT EVEN GETTING A NORMAL X-RAY VIEW OF UNDERGROUND STRATA!

Superman and Supergirl use X-ray vision to fight crime. Real-life heroes like doctors use X-rays to spot broken bones and help heal injured or sick patients.

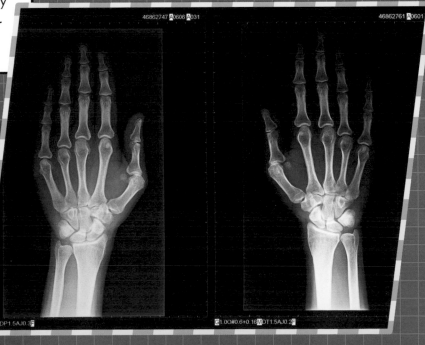

How Can You See IN THE DARK?

Batman does most of his work at night. It's difficult to see at night because there's little light. Humans can only see when there's enough light to bounce off objects and into their eyes. But Batman is prepared for anything. He uses special lenses built into his cowl to let him see even when there's very little light. These goggles work by seeing types of light that human eyes usually can't.

Some night vision goggles can see **INFRARED LIGHT**. Normally, you can't see this type of light. But night vision goggles can detect it. They turn infrared light into electrical signals that the wearer sees as green images.

Until we create the same technology as Batman, night vision goggles will be more like binoculars. Here, they are attached to a soldier's helmet.

The view through night vision goggles always looks green because green light is easier to see in the dark.

But sometimes it's so dark that there's no light at all to pick up on. Not even infrared! Under these conditions, Batman would need night vision goggles that can see **THERMAL ENERGY**. Thermal energy is better known as heat. Anything that gives off heat produces thermal energy—that includes humans! With his ingenious inventions and gadgets, Batman is prepared for nearly anything. No one can take Batman by surprise!

What Could You See if You Had ULTRAVIOLET VISION?

Everything we see is made up of visible light. But there are types of light that our eyes can't see. One of those types of light is **ULTRAVIOLET LIGHT**. Its wavelength is shorter than visible light, but longer than an X-ray. You may not be able to see ultraviolet light, but you've felt it. Ultraviolet light is part of sunlight!

Martian Manhunter isn't human. He's an alien from Mars. And his eyes can see ultraviolet light. To Martian Manhunter, colors look very different. They're brighter and seem to softly glow. Unlike humans eyes, Martian Manhunter's eyes have cones that can detect ultraviolet colors. Some birds and insects can see ultraviolet light too!

This is what a marsh marigold looks like to a human in daylight.

Bees and other insects that look for pollen on flowers can see ultraviolet light. The marsh marigold looks very different to a bee!

Scorpions glow under ultraviolet light. Scientists aren't sure why yet. If only we could ask Martian Manhunter!

BUILD A SPECTROSCOPE

Visible light is made up of every color of the rainbow, or the spectrum of color. When we look at a light source, we can't see all the colors that make up the light.

But you can with a spectroscope! A spectroscope breaks white light into color. It can be used to see how different light sources have different spectra, or color bands.

...FLASH *AND THE* GREEN LANTERN *GATHER WITH* AQUAMAN *ABOUT* SNAPPER...

HIS SPECTRUM SHOWS NOTHING UNUSUAL EXCEPT THE SPECTRO- SCOPIC LINES FOR CALCIUM! IT SHOWS HE'S COVERED WITH CALCIUM OXIDE-- LIME!

THAT FIGURES... I WAS USING LIME ON THE LAWN TODAY...

Green Lantern is using his ring to see the entire spectrum of color coming from the elements on his friend Snapper.

MATERIALS:

Empty cereal box

Scissors

Pencil

Tape

Ruler

A CD or DVD (make sure your parents are OK with you using it!)

Light source (like a lamp or overhead light)

Aluminum foil

1. On the top of the cereal box, measure and mark 1.5 inches from the narrow edge. Put a mark on both flaps.

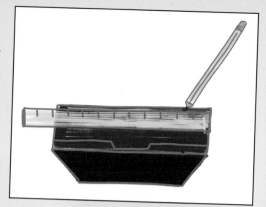

2. Use your ruler to draw a line across the top of the cereal box to connect the marks you made in step 1.

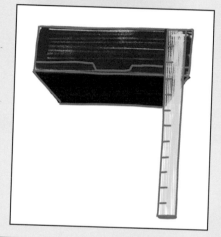

3. Ask an adult for help to carefully cut along this line. This should leave you with three flaps. Cut them off so you have a small rectangular opening on the top edge of the cereal box.

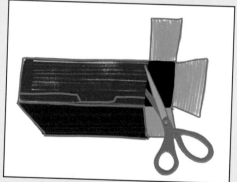

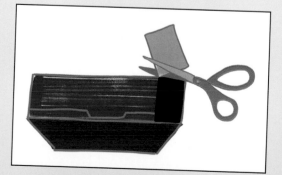

continued on next page

continued from previous page

4. Use your ruler to measure and draw a rectangle that is 1 inch wide and 2 inches tall. Draw a diagonal line from the top corner of the box to the opposite corner of the rectangle. Cut along that line. Repeat on the opposite side of the box.

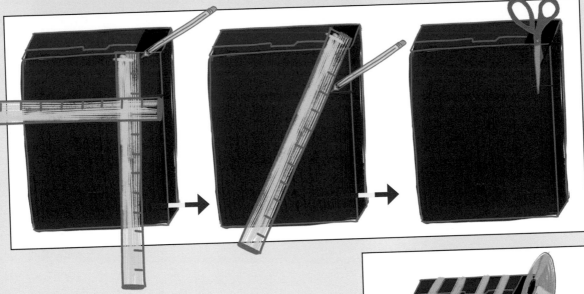

5. Slide the CD into the slits you made. The shiny side should be face-up. Tape the top of the box closed.

6. Cut a hole out of the side of the cereal box on the opposite side from where the CD is placed. The top of the hole should be a half inch from the top of the box. Make the hole about 1 inch tall and about as wide as the side of the box.

7. Take a piece of aluminum foil and fold it in half. Tape it in place over the top half of the hole, with the creased edge across the hole. Take another piece of aluminum foil, fold it, and cover the bottom half of the hole, leaving a tiny gap between the two pieces of aluminum foil. This gap should be very small!

8. Point the small gap at a light source, like a light bulb or computer screen. (Not the sun! You should never look directly at the sun.) Look into the hole on the top of the box. What do you see on the CD?

People use many different types of light bulbs in homes and offices today. CFL (compact fluorescent), LED (light-emitting diode), and incandescent light bulbs are three common types of light bulbs used today. Ask your parents to help you try them all in your experiment.

What's Happening? Your spectroscope will let you see the rainbow of colors hiding in seemingly white light! Look at a variety of light sources, like different types of light bulbs, a candle, a neon sign, or the moon. Each one will have its own spectrum of colors. Are their spectra similar or different? Record your observations.

ACTIVITY

SEEING THE INVISIBLE

Many super heroes have powerful vision. They can see kinds of light that the normal human eye can't see. But with a bit of experimentation, you, too, can see the invisible!

MATERIALS:

Clear nail polish

A small bowl of clean water

Strips of sturdy black paper

1. Observe your clear nail polish in the bottle. Brush a bit of it onto the black paper. What do you see? Can you tell where the nail polish is?

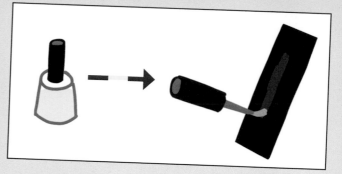

2. Open the clear nail polish. Carefully drop a single drop of nail polish onto the surface of the water.

3. Observe what happens. Can you see where the nail polish is? Does it look different than it did in the bottle or brushed onto the paper?

4. Use your piece of black paper to scoop up the nail polish. What does it look like? What colors do you see?

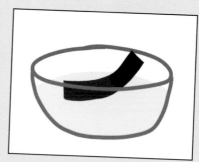

What's Happening? Super heroes can see light at different wavelengths. But so can you! Normally nail polish is a thick coating or film. But when you let a drop of it spread across water, it becomes a thin film. A thin film is only a few nanometers thick—that's ten thousand times smaller than the thickness of your hair! The light can't fully pass through the thin film. Instead, it bounces off early, causing the light to shift wavelengths ever so slightly. This slight shift causes you to see a rainbow of colors where there used to be only a clear film!

ENGINEERING
Building Bigger and Better Things

Engineers build gadgets, buildings, roads, and other things. They are constantly identifying ways to solve problems and improve existing machines and structures.

Engineers build cars, spaceships, skyscrapers, and bridges. They also design cool new things like game consoles and smartphones. If you like building things and finding clever ways to do difficult tasks, you might be an engineer in the making!

Many super heroes are engineers in disguise. Whenever Batman comes up with a new Batarang or special tool to track down a villain, he's working as an engineer. Many civilians who work with super heroes are engineers too. The Justice League's space station headquarters was built by **AEROSPACE** engineers who specialize in space flight. And Commissioner Gordon, of the Gotham City Police Department, invented the Bat-Signal to communicate with Batman. Thinking like an engineer, he saw a problem, and he solved it!

THE BAT-SIGNAL

CARBON ARC FILAMENTS

BATSLIDE

IN THE PAST, HEAVY FOG HAS STYMIED THE USE OF THE *BAT-SIGNAL*. THAT'S ONE OF THE CONDITIONS THIS NEW MODEL WILL CORRECT!

ELECTRONIZED SILVER REFLECTOR

BULLET-PROOF GLASS, HAND-GROUND FOR CLARITY

NEW CHANGEABLE CARRIAGE

BUMBLEBEE,
ENGINEER

Karen Beecher is better known as the super hero Bumblebee. She doesn't have any superpowers like super-strength or laser vision. But that doesn't mean she's powerless! She designed a special suit that lets her shrink, fly, create electric bursts, and move very quickly. Bumblebee was able to do this because she is an **ENGINEER**.

Engineers use math, science, and creativity to create new things and solve problems. Many engineers are inspired by nature. One of the most powerful shapes in nature is the hexagon—the same shape that makes up honeycombs in a beehive! Hexagons have six sides and can neatly be packed together into strong structures. Bees are natural engineers, so it's no wonder Bumblebee was inspired by them!

Bees are some of nature's coolest engineers. They build incredible hives filled with compartments that house their babies and store their honey. Scientists say the repeating pattern of hexagon-shaped structures is hugely efficient. It takes the least amount of wax to build strong, secure walls in this shape. And there are no gaps or wasted space.

What TOOLS and MACHINES Help Engineers Build?

One of the coolest things about super heroes is their super technology! From Wonder Woman's Invisible Jet to Batman's Batmobile, the things super heroes design and build make their jobs easier. If you build something, you're an engineer!

Engineers use simple machines to build complicated objects. Here are some of the simple machines that allow engineers to build everything from a small road to a gigantic opera house.

LEVER: A stick, rod, or plane balanced on a fixed point called a fulcrum. Levers help lift heavy objects more easily.

WHEEL AND AXLE: A wheel is a round object that can roll. It has a center opening that an axle can pass through. An axle is a rod or spindle that the wheel can rotate around. It's what attaches wheels to your bike or car! Together, they help people travel farther and carry loads more easily.

PULLY: A rope draped over a wheel. You pull on one side of the rope to raise the other. Pullies make it easier to lift up objects.

INCLINED PLANE: A slope or ramp. It is easier to move things up an inclined plane than to lift them straight up. Stairs are a type of inclined plane!

WEDGE: A wedge is shaped like two inclined planes put together. Wedges help push objects apart. The narrow side is pushed into an opening. As the wedge moves further into the opening, the opening gets wider.

SCREW: A screw is an inclined plane that's been twisted into a spiral. The shape of a screw helps it work its way into wood or other surfaces.

How Can a Vehicle Be INVISIBLE?

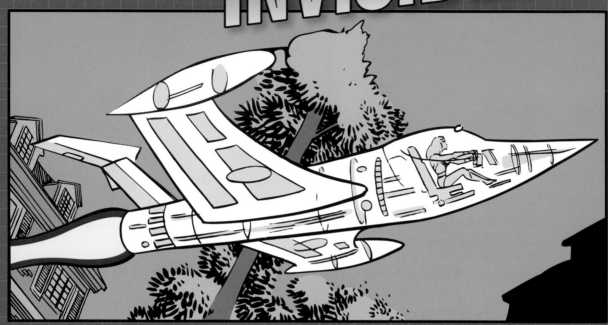

When you fight villains all the time, being able to sneak up on someone is important. Wonder Woman's plane is the sneakiest of them all! Villains can't see her Invisible Jet flying overhead. It lets her get to a secret lair or to a fight without being noticed.

We don't have invisible vehicles, but we can be very sneaky. Some planes are painted dark colors and flown at night to blend in with the night sky. This is a type of **CAMOUFLAGE**. Camouflage is a way of hiding something—like a plane or an animal—by coloring it so it blends in with its surroundings.

Even an invisible plane would still be spotted if it didn't have the right stealth abilities! Planes are detected by **RADAR**. Radar bounces radio waves off objects and back to a detector. The detector can tell how far away the object is and how big it is. As long as it's solid, radar works! But some stealth planes are designed so they're very hard to spot with radar. They absorb or deflect radio waves so they aren't fully detected. They might not be invisible, but they sure are tricky to find!

Scientists in Sweden have developed a way to keep tanks from being located by night vision goggles or infrared sensors (which detect thermal energy, or heat). The engineers cover the tanks with about a thousand little metal panels that can be heated or cooled quickly. Sensors on the tank constantly detect the temperature outside. The machine then mimics, or imitates, the temperature of its surroundings by heating or cooling the panels. Since the tank is the same temperature, infrared sensors can't detect it! It blends right in.

How FAST Is the Batmobile?

IT'S LIGHT AS A FEATHER, *BATMAN*, AND STEADY AS A ROCK!

YOU CAN ACCELER-ATE TO 100 MILES PER HOUR IN 100 FEET, AND STOP ON A DIME!

The Batmobile is a special vehicle that can reach super-high speeds. Most cars can't go 310 miles per hour, but the Batmobile sure can, because it has a special jet turbine engine. Regular cars use a **PISTON ENGINE**. Piston engines spray fuel into the engine, which is then combusted (burned) or exploded. These explosions move a crankshaft, which causes the wheels to move. The engine only powers the wheels for a part of the time, not continuously. A **JET TURBINE ENGINE**, however, constantly produces power by taking in fuel and combusting it simultaneously. That lets the Batmobile travel much faster. Vroooooom!

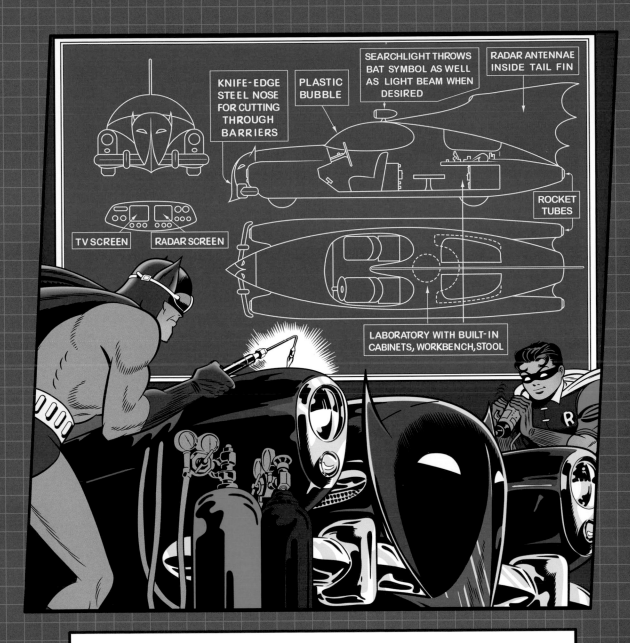

When designing cars, real-life engineers put each vehicle through safety testing. They need to make sure that the car can safely travel at high speeds and that safety features like airbags and seat belts protect passengers. Engineering isn't just about building cool things—it's also about keeping people safe!

Can a Lasso Really Be UNBREAKABLE?

Wonder Woman's Lasso of Truth is incredible. It's a weapon. And it protects anyone standing inside its loop. It can also force anyone to tell the truth. But it cannot be broken.

Scientists have not yet found a substance in real life that can make people tell the truth. But they have invented a nearly indestructible material: **GRAPHENE**.

Graphene is ultra-thin and made from pure carbon. At first, scientists created **2D** graphene. Then they formed 2D graphene into a sponge-like pattern to create **3D** graphene.

2D means something has two dimensions: length and width. In other words, it is flat.

3D means it has three dimensions: length, width, and height.

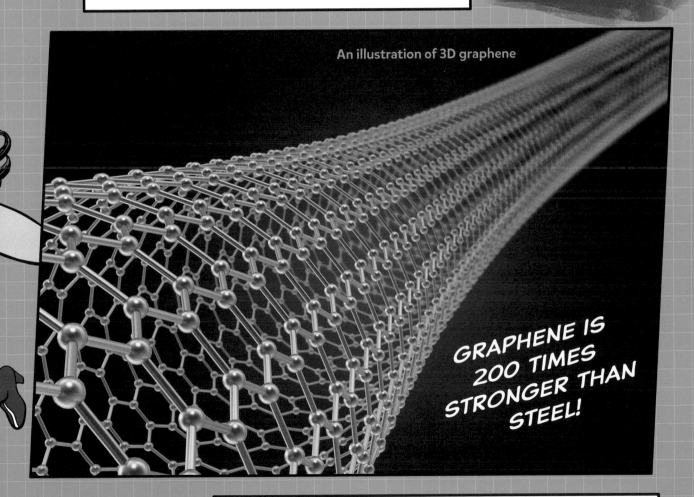

An illustration of 3D graphene

GRAPHENE IS 200 TIMES STRONGER THAN STEEL!

Now a company is trying to create graphene rubber bands. Soon, there may be a substance just as stretchy and unbreakable as Wonder Woman's lasso!

Are CYBORGS Science Fiction?

Victor Stone was a regular high school athlete with a talented scientist father. After he was caught in a laboratory accident, his father used technology to turn him into a **CYBORG**. A cyborg is a person with mechanical parts built into their body. At first, Victor was upset about his new body. But he learned that his mechanical parts let him fight crime and help save the world, and he became the super hero Cyborg.

But cyborgs aren't just found in comic books. People with **PROSTHETIC** limbs use technology as part of their body. They can walk or grab things with their mechanical parts. Some people use cochlear implants to hear or pacemakers to keep their heart beating steadily. They may not turn people into super heroes, but cyborg parts save lives every day!

PROSTHETIC refers to any artificial body part, such as a hand, leg, or even a heart.

Prosthetic limbs can help people who have lost body parts due to injury or disease. There are many different kinds of prosthesis. Recently, scientists and everyday people have been experimenting with using 3D printers to make low-cost prosthetic devices.

PAPER PLANE SHOWDOWN

You can't build your own plane just yet. But you can fold one out of paper! Test out three different paper plane designs. Observe how each one flies, how far it goes, and even how fast. Then see if you can design a better paper airplane!

MATERIALS:

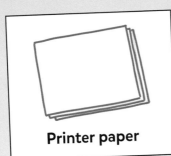

Printer paper

Painter's tape (or masking tape)

Optional: Measuring tape, stopwatch

1. Fold a **BASIC PAPER AIRPLANE.**

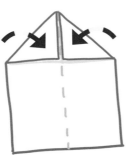

1. Fold the paper in half. Make a crease. Then open it up again.

2. Fold down the corners so they meet at the center crease.

3. Fold the paper in half.

4. Fold the top flap down to meet the center crease. Repeat on the other side.

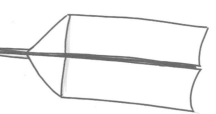

5. Pull up the flaps. Position the wings so your plane is ready to fly.

2

2. Fold a BASIC DART AIRPLANE.

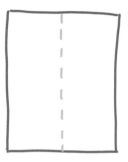 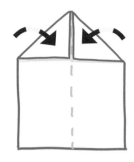 

1. Fold the paper in half. Make a crease. Then open it up again.

2. Fold down the corners so they meet at the center crease.

3. Fold the right side of the paper in half again so it reaches the center crease. Repeat on the other side.

4. Fold the paper in half along the center crease.

5. Fold the top flap down to meet the center crease. Repeat on the other side.

6. Pull up the flaps. Position the wings so your plane is ready to fly.

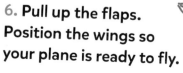

continued on next page

continued from previous page

3. Fold a STABLE AIRPLANE.

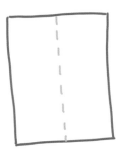 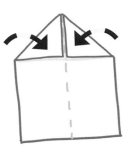  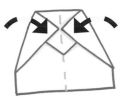

1. Fold the paper in half. Make a crease. Then open it up again.

2. Fold down the corners so they meet at the center crease.

3. Fold the point down to meet the center crease.

4. Fold the top right corner in to meet the center crease. Repeat with the top left corner.

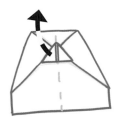  

5. Fold the downward-facing point (from step 3) up.

6. Fold the paper in half (the opposite way from the initial crease in step 1).

7. Fold the top flap down to reach the center crease. Repeat with the other side.

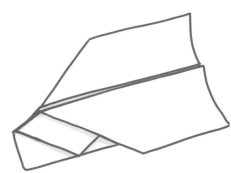

8. Pull up the flaps. Position the wings so your plane is ready to fly.

4. Mark a line on the floor with painter's tape. Launch each airplane one by one from the line. Make sure you don't cross it—that would give one type of airplane an unfair advantage!

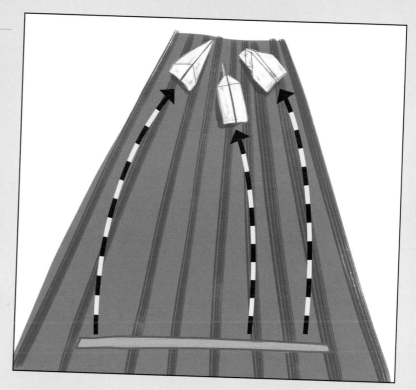

5. Make a note of how each one flies. Which one flies the farthest? What about that design do you think helped it fly the way that it did?

What's Happening? The way you folded the paper airplane changed how **AERODYNAMIC** it was. An object is aerodynamic when it reduces drag from the air moving past it. The more aerodynamic the plane, the farther and straighter it will fly. Which of your paper airplanes do you think was the most aerodynamic?

Use your creativity and keep folding new planes. Think like an engineer and try to design your own paper airplane that can fly even farther or faster!

DANGER IN NATURE

Risks Lurking in the Wild

Even super heroes have weaknesses. Superman becomes weak near Kryptonite, Batman is susceptible to poison, and Starfire needs sunlight. We have weaknesses, too—and some of them are the same as our favorite heroes'. Certain things in nature, like rare rocks and poisonous plants, can hurt us. These things cause us harm by interacting with our bodies. When

we touch these things, we can have an allergic reaction. You might break out in an itchy rash as your body's immune system rushes to push away the substance.

Even the weather can put you in harm's way! Extreme heat might cause you to become dehydrated, which is when you lose too much water. And extreme cold can lead to frostbite.

It's fun to explore and play outdoors, but safety should always come first! Be like a super hero and be prepared for anything by being familiar with your surroundings.

Superman's icy Fortress of Solitude gives him plenty of privacy, but if he didn't have his tolerance for cold, it would be too dangerous to visit the Fortress without plenty of warm layers!

Can Plants Be DEADLY?

Poison Ivy is an expert on plants. She can make anything grow! Many of her plants are **POISONOUS**. When super heroes like Batman are exposed to them, they get hurt. Her plants can cause rashes, sleepiness, or even make it hard to move! But is Poison Ivy's villainous vegetation fact or fiction?

Fact! Many plants you can find in the real world have nasty effects. Poison Ivy's namesake is common and causes an itchy rash. If you come across a plant in the wild that you don't recognize, don't touch it! Better safe than sorry with these sneaky species.

POISON IVY is a common plant found in woody areas. Just brushing against it can result in a red, itchy rash.

The innocent-looking bell-shaped flowers of the **LILY OF THE VALLEY** can cause dizziness and nausea.

In large amounts, **HYDRANGEA** flowers can become a source of the deadly poison cyanide.

MISTLETOE is a holiday favorite. But don't eat it! It can cause hallucinations.

POISON IVY,
BOTANIST

Poison Ivy knows a lot about plants. That's because she's a **BOTANIST**. Botanists study all kinds of plants. They work to understand how plants grow and what unique properties they have. Some botanists work on special food for plants, called fertilizer, to help plants grow better. A botanist might also work with farmers to develop crops that can handle extreme weather or resist illnesses. Others specialize in specific plants, like redwood trees in California, and study how those plants are reacting to climate change.

Many botanists are also environmentalists—including Poison Ivy! Environmentalists want to protect nature. Some botanists work to make sure rare plants don't go **EXTINCT**. When a plant goes extinct, it can no longer be found anywhere in the world. Botanists grow rare plants in greenhouses, labs, and gardens to make sure they keep growing for many years to come.

Some botanists are helping astronauts grow plants in space. Talk about out-of-this-world cabbage!

Is KRYPTONITE Real?

Just being near Kryptonite makes Superman weak. And, if he were exposed to it long enough, it could even kill him. Kryptonite was formed by the radiation of his home planet Krypton when it exploded. But the planet Krypton and the dangerous rocks called Kryptonite only *really* exist in the comics. What about here on Earth? Are there rocks in nature that can be dangerous for you, like the radiation from Kryptonite is dangerous to Superman?

Yes! There are. (But don't worry. Unless you are mining deep in the earth, climbing around volcanoes, or working with nuclear waste, you won't stumble across them. Here are a few **DANGEROUS MINERALS**.

CINNABAR can be found near volcanoes and hot springs. When it is heated up or disturbed, it can give off deadly mercury.

TORBERNITE is a rare, bright green crystal found in some granite rocks. It can release a gas that can give people lung cancer.

For many years, people ground **STIBNITE** into a dark powder and used it as makeup. It was also used to make eating utensils . . . until scientists discovered it could poison people. Oops!

CREATE AN OUTDOOR SAFETY GUIDEBOOK

ACTIVITY

Super heroes pay attention to their surroundings. They take note of the animals and plants in an area. This helps them stay safe. They can avoid dangerous animals or plants with thorns or other defenses.

Super heroes are always prepared—and you can be too! One way you can be prepared is by creating a guidebook.

MATERIALS:

Construction paper

Markers or colored pencils

A stapler

Research materials such as books on plants and animals

1. Stack a few sheets of paper on top of each other. Fold them in half vertically, like a book.

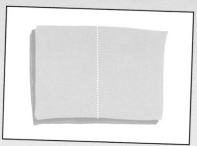

2. Staple along the edge of the fold. You've made a book!

3. Come up with a title for your guidebook. Write it on the front of your book. And don't forget to include your name!

4. On each page, draw a type of plant or animal that lives in your state. Write down important information, such as how big it is and whether it's poisonous or venomous. (Something that is poisonous can make an animal sick if it is eaten or if its poisons are absorbed into the skin. Venomous animals, like snakes or bees, bite or sting in order to inject poisons through a wound.)

What's Happening? A guidebook has important information about your surroundings in it. It can be an important reference when you're out in the wild—or just in your backyard. If you see a plant or animal you don't recognize, look it up. You can always add more pages to your book!

INDEX